ALBERT P. RYDER

Albert P.
RYDER

by Lloyd Goodrich

GEORGE BRAZILLER, INC.
NEW YORK   1959

LIBRARY OF CONGRESS CATALOG CARD NUMBER: 59-12227

PRINTED IN THE UNITED STATES OF AMERICA
BY R. R. DONNELLEY & SONS COMPANY

CONTENTS

ACKNOWLEDGEMENTS

THE AUTHOR wishes to record his indebtedness to the many individuals who through the years have rendered generous assistance to his research on Ryder's life and work; especially to Mrs. Charles de Kay, Philip Evergood, Mr. and Mrs. Edward D. Gurney, Mrs. Rosalie Warner Jones, Kenneth Hayes Miller, Mrs. Lloyd Williams and Mrs. Dorothy Weir Young, all of whom furnished essential personal information and documents; to Mrs. Frederic Fairchild Sherman, who generously donated the material used by Mr. Sherman in writing the first book published on Ryder; to Sheldon Keck of the Brooklyn Museum for invaluable co-operation in scientific examination of paintings; to Murray Pease and F. du Pont Cornelius of the Metropolitan Museum, and Thomas M. Beggs of the National Collection of Fine Arts, for assistance in securing x-rays; to Carmine Dalesio of the Babcock Galleries, for his constant interest and help in all matters connected with Ryder; and to Miss Lelia Wittler, William F. Davidson and Miss Elizabeth Clare of M. Knoedler & Co., Robert G. McIntyre of William Macbeth, Inc., Albert and Harold Milch and Joseph Gotlieb of E. & A. Milch, Inc., and Robert C. Vose of the Vose Galleries, for their valuable information on paintings which have passed through their hands. Special thanks are due also to Rosalind Irvine, Curator of the Whitney Museum of American Art, who prepared the bibliography; to John I. H. Baur, Associate Director of the Museum, for his constant cooperation in examining paintings; and to the author's secretary, Frances Manola, for her un-failing help in research and writing. Grateful acknowledgment is made to the Whitney Museum for its kind permission to use portions of the author's text of the catalogue of the Ryder Centenary Exhibition in 1947.

L.G.

ALBERT P. RYDER

Photograph by Alice Boughton, Courtesy of the Library of Congress

THE AMERICAN MIND is generally thought of as practical, matter-of-fact and extroverted. Certainly these are conspicuous traits in our national character. In our art the most common trend up to the present century was naturalism. But equally characteristic, if not as frequent, was the dark vein of romanticism. In literature it produced Poe, Hawthorne, Melville and Emily Dickinson. In painting it began with Benjamin West, Washington Allston and others who attempted the Grand Style, and was continued in a more naturalistic style by the Hudson River School, with their huge canvases celebrating the wonders and beauties of the continent. By the last third of the nineteenth century the old grandiose romantic tradition had run its course, and was giving way to the more personal, intimate romanticism of Inness, Hunt, Fuller, Newman, La Farge, Blakelock and Ryder. Of all these, the most original figure was that of Albert Ryder.

Ryder's art was a product of an intense inner life, little influenced by the world around him or the art of others. In it the dead wood of the older romantic school was eliminated—the nostalgia for Italy and the old masters that had devitalized the exponents of the Grand Style, the literalism that had encumbered the Hudson River School. Ryder pictured the inner reality of the mind, and out of this deep unconscious world brought forth the purest poetic imagery in our art of the century. In form and design he was the most original plastic artist of his time. The romantic imagination which had been starved or misdirected in so many of his predecessors found full ex-

11

pression, in stranger form but with greater intensity, in the work of our first pure imaginative creator.

II

ALBERT PINKHAM RYDER was descended from old Cape Cod families on both his father's and mother's sides. The Ryders or Riders had been settled since the middle seventeenth century at Yarmouth on the north shore of the Cape. His grandfather Benjamin Ryder was a carpenter who built several houses in the town; he and his wife were religious, belonging to a strict Methodist sect whose women dressed Quaker-fashion. The artist's father, Alexander Gage Ryder, was born at Yarmouth in 1815, and married Elizabeth Cobb of New Bedford, granddaughter of Judge Daniel Davis of Barnstable on the Cape, an eminent Massachusetts jurist. An early account says that she was "distinguished for benevolence, self-sacrifice and sympathy —a beautiful woman with a beautiful character. It has been said of Albert Ryder's genius that he owed it to his mother, a passionate lover of flowers and beautiful things." About 1840 the family moved to New Bedford, where Alexander Ryder became a dealer in fuel and also boarding officer at the port.

The future artist, youngest of four brothers, was born in New Bedford, March 19, 1847, in an old house opposite the home of Albert Bierstadt's family. At this time New Bedford was at the height of its activity as the greatest whaling port in the world. Many of the Ryder family had followed the sea; so did two of Albert's brothers, and a favorite childhood memory was of one of them coming home from a long voyage and in his happiness kissing the pig. From earliest consciousness the sea must have played a large part in Ryder's life. His bent toward art showed early. "When he was only four years old," his sister-in-law said, "he would be found lying on his stomach on the floor, lost to the world in his picture book. He did not care so much about drawing, as long as he had his colors."

He graduated from a local grammar school but did not go beyond, as his eyesight had been impaired. All his life his eyes troubled him; if he painted too long they became inflamed. For a while he worked in what the early accounts vaguely call "commercial life." He began painting by himself, without regular instruction, though helped somewhat by an amateur artist of the town. In later life he described his youthful struggles: "Nature is a teacher who never deceives. When I grew weary with the futile struggle to imitate the canvases of the past, I went out into the fields, determined to serve nature as faithfully as I had served art. In my desire to be accurate I became lost in a maze of detail. Try as I would, my colors were not those of nature. My leaves were infinitely below the standard of a leaf, my finest strokes were coarse and crude. The old scene presented itself one day before my eyes framed in an opening between two trees. It stood out like a painted canvas—the deep blue of a midday sky—a solitary tree, brilliant with the green of early summer, a foundation of brown earth and gnarled roots. There was no detail to vex the eye. Three solid masses of form and color—sky, foliage and earth—the whole bathed in an atmosphere of golden luminosity. I threw my brushes aside; they were too small for the work in hand. I squeezed out big chunks of pure, moist color and taking my palette knife, I laid on blue, green, white and brown in great sweeping strokes. As I worked I saw that it was good and clean and strong. I saw nature springing into life upon my dead canvas. It was better than nature, for it was vibrating with the thrill of a new creation. Exultantly I painted until the sun sank below the horizon, then I raced around the fields like a colt let loose, and literally bellowed for joy."*

His brother William had moved to New York, become proprietor of a restaurant, and prospered; and about 1870 his father and mother and Albert followed. New York was to be his home the rest of his life. He applied for admission to the school of the National

* This and other long quotations from Ryder were published in "Paragraphs from the Studio of a Recluse" in the *Broadway Magazine*, September, 1905. Ryder wrote Prof. John Pickard in 1907: "In the paragraphs from a studio you will find what is practically an interview by Miss Adelaide Samson, now Mrs. Maundy; it was done from memory: and gives a wrong impression in the instance of copying old masters: otherwise quite correct." (*Art in America*, April, 1939.)

Academy of Design, but was rejected. About this time he was befriended by William E. Marshall, a portraitist and engraver who had studied under the French academician Couture, who had been Manet's master. Marshall specialized in portraits of famous men, painstaking and unsophisticated though good in character; but he also painted some romantic and religious subjects that make one understand why Ryder was attracted to him. Marshall encouraged him to persevere working on his own and bringing his pictures to him for criticism. After a while Ryder applied again to the Academy and was admitted. The instruction at this time was chiefly in drawing from casts, and Ryder probably got less out of this than from the informal teaching of Marshall, who he said "remained my friendly critic for some time."

Ryder never dated his paintings—indeed, he frequently did not even sign them—and many of them he worked on for years. So the chronology of his work is hard to fix. But some of his early exhibits can be identified, and we have titles and sometimes brief descriptions of others. Judging from this, his paintings of the 1870's were mostly landscapes, often with figures or with horses and cattle, smaller and more naturalistic than his later pictures. His friend Charles de Kay wrote in 1890 that he had "won his fame chiefly as a landscapist up to a recent time."

These early landscapes and farm scenes are reminiscences of the country around New Bedford, with its secluded stony pastures, old stone walls and wood lots. The young artist's affection for animals shows in his grazing cows, horses and sheep. The hours are seldom full daylight, but late golden afternoon, sunset, twilight or moonlight. The spirit is idyllic: *The Sheepfold* (plate 3) with huddled sheep in the moonlight and lighted cottage windows, *Moonrise* with the dark form of an alarmed wandering cow, or *Homeward Plodding,* a farmer driving home in the twilight, are in the mood of Gray's *Elegy in a Country Churchyard.* Sometimes, as in *Spring* (plate 5), a female figure introduces a semi-allegorical note. The pastoral poetry of these pictures reminds one of William Blake and his followers such as Samuel Palmer and Edward Calvert. There is a strangeness in them; they seem memories of the landscapes of

14

childhood, transformed by the mind into images akin to those in dreams. The style is of almost childlike simplicity, giving only essentials. The revelation that came to Ryder in the fields remained with him; the whole picture is seen in a few large masses and colors, and, as he said, "bathed in an atmosphere of golden luminosity." Everything is conceived in color and tone, but the forms are definite and full of an odd, original character. Here was an utterly personal art, product of a mind that lived in a world of its own—a mind as self-sufficient as that other New Englander, Emily Dickinson. Its intimate poetry was at the opposite extreme from the huge literal panoramas of the Hudson River School, then at its zenith.

Ryder exhibited for the first time, as far as we know, at the National Academy in the spring of 1873, when he was twenty-six; but he was included only once in the next seven years. At this time the Academy, which held the only important exhibitions in New York, was under the absolute control of the old-line academicians, to whom Delacroix and even Corot were still revolutionaries. But a younger generation trained in Munich or Paris was beginning to return, with freer ideas. The Academy refused to adapt itself to these innovators, and soon there was open warfare. Ryder found himself aligned with the men of the "New Movement," as it was called. About 1875, he and four other painters, all of whom had been rejected by the Academy, were invited by Cottier & Co., the English firm which recently had started a New York branch, to hold an exhibition there. The show roused much interest and was one of the factors leading to the founding in 1877 of a rival to the Academy, the Society of American Artists, which was to be the outstanding liberal artists' organization for the next two decades. Ryder was one of its twenty-two founders and remained a member as long as it lasted. It was his chief exhibiting medium; he showed in the first nine exhibitions, from 1878 to 1887, often several pictures at a time. William C. Brownell wrote in 1880: "If it had not been for the Society of American Artists it is doubtful whether such an unmistakably genuine painter as Mr. A. P. Ryder would ever have had his pictures hung where they could be seen." However, he managed to

15

get a picture into the Academy almost every year during the 1880's, though he was not elected even an Associate until 1902, the same year as Eakins, and an Academician until 1906, when the two societies merged. He exhibited a good deal more in the 1880's than at any other period, though not nearly as much as many contemporaries now forgotten.

Up to about the age of forty he received little attention from critics. Amid the spectacular canvases of the Hudson River School or the dashing brushwork of the Munich men, his modest paintings were passed over in silence or with a bare mention. Sometimes he was singled out for attack, usually along with Ralph Albert Blakelock, mistakenly called his pupil. The chief complaints raised were the liberties both took with "nature." A critic in 1880 advised them to try "the hard, grinding, sweaty toil of academic drawing and accurate anatomy," and another in 1883 admonished: "Come out into the clear light, gentlemen! Show what you can do in the glare of day! See whether your poetry is strong enough, healthy enough, to stand the wear and tear of life!" But not all the critics were hostile; some were attracted by Ryder's sentiment and color, though all deplored his supposed lack of form. On the whole his reception was better than poor Blakelock's, in both criticism and opportunities to exhibit.

Most of the personal accounts we have of Ryder, as of many a man who achieves fame late, are of him in later years, when he had become eccentric. Of what kind of young man he was, there are fewer accounts. In person he was fairly tall and inclined to be heavy, with a full reddish-brown beard even as a young man. An early photograph shows a fine high forehead, a strong, well-modeled nose, fair skin, eyes sensitive and full of reverie—a remarkable face, combining strength and sensibility. The sculptor James E. Kelly, a fellow student at the Academy, speaks of his sweet voice and gentle smile, and says, "At that time he was very neat, with a New England regard for the proprieties."

Though shy, he had a sweetness of nature that brought him many friends. In young manhood he seems to have been normally sociable. Among his closest friends, who remained so all their lives,

16

were his dealer, Daniel Cottier, and the latter's partner, James S. Inglis, the painter J. Alden Weir, the sculptor Olin L. Warner and the critic Charles de Kay. In a letter from London to William R. Mead, the architect, Ryder sends remembrances to "White and McKim, and Maynard, and Weir, and Lathrop, and Warner and everybody"—scarcely the letter of a hermit. A friend of Cottier's, Captain John Robinson of the Atlantic Transport Line, who knew Ryder well in the 1880's and 1890's, wrote: "I have read of Ryder being a recluse. I can hardly think that, for the small luncheon and dinner parties, where a few friends met, were never complete without him. He never talked much; he was an excellent listener, and his laugh was very infectious."

Until over thirty he lived with his family, and was probably helped financially by his brother William, the money-maker of the family. About 1880 he set up for himself in the Benedick Building on East Washington Square, bachelor home of many fellow artists, where he lived and worked for over ten years.

He made several trips abroad. The first was in 1877, for a month's stay in London. In the summer of 1882 he and Daniel Cottier toured England, and later, in company with Warner, the Continent, visiting France, Holland, Italy, Spain and Tangier. De Kay called this "a hurried trip" and said: "What is most curious is the little liking he showed for travel, the strong dislike for hurry, the comparative weakness of the impression made on him by the old galleries, and his almost complete rejection of modern art in Europe. To his companions this natural chauvinism was entertaining." At thirty-five, with his highly personal introspective temperament fully developed, Ryder was evidently not a good subject for the Grand Tour. What made the most lasting impression was his visit, perhaps on this trip, to the studio of Matthew Maris, with whom he had many affinities in both his art and his way of living, and for whom he retained a lifelong admiration.

Twice again he crossed the Atlantic, in 1887 and 1896. On these occasions he went just for the sea voyage, each time on his friend Captain Robinson's ship, spending only a couple of weeks in London and returning on the same ship. His foreign experience was thus much less than that of most of his American contemporaries, even of Homer and Eakins; and it had little effect on his artistic knowledge or taste.

III

IN HIS EARLY thirties, after about 1880, Ryder struck out from his early relatively naturalistic landscapes and idyllic scenes into more imaginative fields. For many of his subjects he drew on the Bible, on classical mythology and on the great poetical literature of the English-speaking world—Chaucer, Shakespeare (his favorite poet), the early ballads and the nineteenth-century romantics—Byron, Moore, Campbell, Poe, Tennyson. Two of his finest paintings were inspired by Wagner's operas, *The Flying Dutchman* and *Götter-dämmerung*. Sometimes he took from literature only a title for his picture, as *With Sloping Mast and Dipping Prow* (plate 31) from *The Ancient Mariner*. But often the theme was purely personal. His simpler fantasies such as his marines had no literary sources, and one of his most extraordinary conceptions, *The Race Track* (plate 69), resulted from the suicide of a friend who had lost his life's savings on a horse race.

Ryder's paintings were never literary in the ordinary sense, never merely illustrations of scenes from books. They were pictorial dramas inspired by great themes, and the themes were transformed into highly personal conceptions, freely interpreted. In all of them nature played an essential part. In *Macbeth and the Witches* (plate 74) the blasted heath under the wind-torn moonlit sky is not a mere background, it is the chief actor, as eloquent of dread and doom as the human actors. In *Siegfried and the Rhine Maidens* (plate 62) the wild agonized movements of the trees are as expressive as the gestures of the tragic hero and the maidens. In *The Forest of Arden* (plate 78) Rosalind and Celia move under the enchantment of the landscape's unearthly beauty. In *Jonah* (plate 45) the ship is a helpless part of the elemental turmoil of the waves. To Ryder, as to all true romantics, nature was not a cold

18

external phenomenon, but an embodiment of man's subjective self, a projection of his emotions of ecstasy, fear and wonder.

Recurring continually in Ryder's art one finds memories of his early contact with the sea. The sea, which has always meant so much to New England, haunted this transplanted New Englander. He never forgot its vastness, its eternal rhythmic flow, the majesty of its storms, its loneliness and terror, and its profound peace. In his frequent concept of a lone boat sailing moonlit waters he gives us the sea as it lives in the mind, an image of infinity and eternity, amid which the boat seems a symbol of man's journey through the unknown. These little marines have a sense of infinite space. They are the most profound sea poems in our art, as Winslow Homer's are the most vigorous sea prose. Of all American artists of their time, these two New Englanders, otherwise so completely different, were our greatest interpreters of the sea.

But Ryder was more than a simple nature poet. In his greatest conceptions, the human or the superhuman are the center. Often the human being is shown at the peril of nature's forces, but under divine guardianship, as in *Jonah,* where God is visibly watching over his prophet, or in *Constance* (plate 65), based on Chaucer's tale, in which the mother and child, cast adrift in their sailless, rudderless boat, are miraculously preserved and guided toward home. To Ryder such themes were not outworn academic motifs, but living poetic truth. He was one of the few authentic religious painters of his period—one of the few in whom religion was not mere conformity, but deep personal emotion. The life of Christ moved him to some of his most tender and impressive works. Though his art lacked the tremendous range of a Delacroix, it had the belief, the unconsciousness and the emotional depth of the great age of romanticism, of which he was a true if belated son.

Ryder was a visionary, one who lived in a dream world, and for whom this world was more real than his actual surroundings. One hesitates to use the word "dream," it has been so sentimentalized; but in the psychological sense of imagery produced not by the intellect operating on external phenomena, but imagery arising from the unconscious mind, his art was literally the representation

19

of dreams. Within his mind actuality went through a long process of transformation, emerging as the inner image of the mind's eye, purified of everything accidental and meaningless. His art carries the conviction of something seen and experienced, which gives it an intense and haunting reality. This integrity of the inward image is a quality as precious as it is rare in modern art. It set Ryder apart not only from the prevailing naturalism of his day, but from the more literary and sentimental romanticism.

Except in his early years he seldom if ever painted directly from nature. But he did much looking at and absorbing of nature, and with all his remoteness from ordinary realism there was a definite element of naturalism in his work. His skies with their strange cloud shapes were well observed, and few have painted moonlight so accurately—the way it mutes colors without effacing them, and the subtle unity of tone it imparts to all things visible. In early years he had pictured relatively realistic light, sometimes even sunlight, as in *Summer's Fruitful Pasture* (plate 9), but as time passed he painted more and more "a light that never was on sea or land." In *The Race Track* the light is that which we experience in dreams—we cannot say whether it is night or day. Indeed, when the owner of the picture asked him which it was, he said, "I hadn't thought about it." Yet his vision was in essential harmony with natural laws; his distortions seem to have been largely unconscious.

But he was never bound by the doctrine of literal faithfulness to nature that governed his older American contemporaries. As he said: "The artist should fear to become the slave of detail. He should strive to express his thought and not the surface of it. What avails a storm cloud accurate in form and color if the storm is not therein?" He used the elements of nature far more freely than any American of his time. He simplified them to their essentials, to what was purely expressive; and he remoulded them, making them obey the rhythms of his instinctive sense of design. Note how the lines of the ship in *Jonah* are distorted out of all relation to nautical accuracy, making it an integral part of the extraordinary turmoil of the sea. His art had no element of mere dead representation; it was all purely plastic. To Ryder painting was a physical language speaking directly to the senses, and his most unearthly concepts were embodied in the sensuous medium of form, color and pigment.

With all the childlike simplicity of his style, verging on the primitive, everything in his pictures had definite form. The tone might be dark, the edges imprecise, but the core of the form was solid and sculptural. Things were seen in masses rather than outlines. Ryder had a passion for form such as other artists have only for color; his forms were strange and original in character, sensuously rich and filled with inner life. He possessed that rare gift, a sense of rhythmic movement. Every line and shape had a vital flow, and was related to every other line and shape. Above all, he had a sense of the harmony of the whole picture. All elements played their parts in a total design that seemed as inevitable as a work of nature. These qualities place him among the purest plastic creators of his period in any country.

In contrast to the brilliancy of his contemporaries the impressionists, his color was prevailingly dark, but with great depth and quiet richness. It was not remarkable for wide range; some of his finest effects were achieved in works that were almost monochromes, by the masterly use of closely related tones. His highly developed sense of color relations gave each painting a chromatic harmony like that of a musical composition.

Ryder's plastic achievements seem to have been purely instinctive rather than based on theory or study of the old masters. The painter Kenneth Hayes Miller, who knew him well in later life, said that his talk about art was entirely concerned with subject and sentiment, not with strictly esthetic qualities. His concepts took shape slowly; he once said, "I've carried the idea for some of my pictures around in my mind for five years before I began to put them on canvas." Walter Pach wrote of him in 1911: "According to his own statement, Mr. Ryder uses no sketches from nature, but lays the picture in according to what he feels to be its needs. Then follows a process of small or large changes that frequently extends over a period of years. The position of clouds in a sky, the contour of a hill, or the movement of a figure undergo infinite modifications until the stability and harmony of masses is attained that the artist's astonishing sense of their beauty demands. 'I work altogether from my feeling for these things, I have no rule. And I think it is better to get the design first before I try for the color. It would be wasted, much of the time, when I have to change things about.'" Of one painting he said to Pach, "Perhaps you wouldn't say it had much drawing, but I think it has what you might call an air of drawing."

He worked long over his pictures, often keeping them in his studio for years, painting on them intermittently, constantly enriching and refining them, trying to bring them nearer a perfection of tone, color and form relationships. As he said: "Art is long. The artist must buckle himself with infinite patience. His ears must be deaf to the clamor of insistent friends who would quicken his pace. His eyes must see naught but the vision beyond. He must await the season of fruitage without haste, without worldly ambitions, without vexation of spirit. An inspiration is no more than a seed that must be planted and nourished.

"The canvas I began ten years ago I shall perhaps complete today or to-morrow. It has been ripening under the sunlight of the years that come and go. . . . It is a wise artist who knows when to cry 'halt' in his composition, but it should be pondered over in his heart and worked out with prayer and fasting."

In reply to a buyer who begged for a painting that had been in process for years, he wrote, quoting Browning:

> *Oh, the little more, and how much it is!*
> *And the little less; and what worlds away!*

To another he wrote: "Have you ever seen an inch worm crawl up a leaf or a twig, and then clinging to the very end, revolve in the air, feeling for something to reach something? That's like me. I am trying to find something out there beyond the place on which I have a footing."

In his whole lifetime he painted only about a hundred and sixty pictures, of which many were small or unfinished and only a relatively few could be called "important." But these alone are enough to secure his fame.

His technical methods were complex. In a day when impressionism and the cult of the clever brush had destroyed traditional methods and substituted direct painting, he strove, half-consciously and without adequate training, for the richness of the old masters. His pictures were built up with underpainting and layer on layer of pigment and glazes, until even a tiny canvas weighs heavy in the hand. He was aiming for the utmost substance, depth and richness of surface, and his most successful works achieve these qualities as few modern paintings have. They have a sensuous richness like enamel, lacquer or pottery.

Unfortunately he had little knowledge of traditional techniques, and in trying to secure his effects he used dangerously unsound methods. He painted over pictures when they were still wet, thereby locking the undersurface in before it had dried and hardened, so that the different surfaces dried at different rates of speed, causing serious cracking. He used strange mediums—wax, candlegrease, alcohol; and he made much too free use of varnish. In showing visitors his paintings he would wipe them with a wet cloth or literally pour varnish over them. As a result almost all his pictures have deteriorated to some extent, many have had to be extensively restored, and a few have been completely ruined. In old age he spent some time trying to repair the damage, but when the artist Salvator Guarino asked him if it did not bother him, he replied: "When a thing has the elements of beauty from the beginning it cannot be destroyed. Take for instance Greek sculpture—the Venus de Milo I might say—ages and men have ravaged it, its arms and nose have been knocked off, but still it remains a thing of beauty because beauty was with it from the beginning." True as this is, it is still one of the tragedies of modern art that Ryder did not have sounder technical knowledge.

With few artists is the favorite scholarly game of tracing influences so unrewarding. He visited museums hardly at all, dealers' galleries occasionally. Miller said that he talked little about other artists and never about the old masters. Corot was his greatest love, and after him Matthew Maris; these were the only two he spoke much about. His work has often been likened to Monticelli's, but when Marshall in the 1870's took him to a Monticelli exhibition at Cottier's and pointed out similarities, it turned out that Ryder had never heard of the French painter.

On this subject Ryder himself said: "Imitation is not inspiration, and inspiration only can give birth to a work of art. The least of a man's original emanation is better than the best of a borrowed thought. In pure perfection of technique, coloring and composition, the art that has already been achieved may be imitated, but never surpassed. Modern art must strike out from the old and assert its individual right to live through Twentieth Century impressionism and interpretation. The new is not revealed to those whose eyes are fastened in worship upon the old. The artist of to-day must work with his face turned toward the dawn, steadfastly believing that his dream will come true before the setting of the sun." And of his beginnings as a painter he said: "When my father placed a box of colors and brushes in my hands, and I stood before my easel with its square of stretched canvas, I realized that I had in my possession the wherewith to create a masterpiece that would live throughout the coming ages. The great masters had no more." Speaking of the old masters, he once said to Miller: "They were great painters, but one can still be an artist."

As Ryder's work matured in the 1880's it met with a somewhat more favorable reception. Influential in this were Daniel Cottier and James Inglis, who bought several of his pictures, interested the few collectors then concerned with American art, and as Ryder said, "had a marked influence on my career." The pioneer collector of native art, Thomas B. Clarke, in 1885 bought two important pictures, *The Temple of the Mind* (plate 36) and *Christ Appearing to Mary* (plate 33). Ryder wrote him: "I find myself so childish in a way; I am so upset with a little appreciation that I can hardly be quiet to acknowledge the source.... For a long time I have observed a marked change in the attitude not only of the press but also of collectors toward the possibilities of something being done here amongst us: to you much of the credit belongs: and I am so happy to be identified with your mission, and that, with the two chief efforts of my ambition. I can not but feel some way that in both the Temple and the religious picture I have gone a little higher up on the mountain and can see other peaks showing along the horizon."

His prices, judging from the few that are known, remained low until his later years. Those given in the exhibition catalogues of the 1880's ranged from $250 to $500. Charles de Kay wrote in 1890: "Ryder has little financial fame. Art dealers for the most part shrug their shoulders over his pictures. . . . It is one of the best signs in Mr. Ryder that he appears little disquieted by the narrowness of the circle to which he now appeals. He declined a dealer's offer to pay liberally for ten pictures to be completed in three years, though ready money was sorely needed."

After 1887 he exhibited only once at the Society of American Artists, and after 1888 never again at the Academy. In later years the few times his pictures were shown were mostly when they were borrowed from collectors. In the 1890's they appeared hardly anywhere except in occasional loan exhibits at New York clubs such as the Lotos and Union League, where they were seen only by a limited public. As he could undoubtedly have gotten them into the Society of American Artists if he had wanted to, it is evident that after forty he ceased to be interested in exhibiting.

The tone of criticism began to be a little more favorable in the early 1880's, his strongest champion being Charles de Kay, who in 1890 published in *The Century* the first full-length article on him. But as his more imaginative works appeared they were generally met with ridicule or incomprehension, as from the writer in 1890 who said that *Jonah* "was chiefly remarkable for the bad taste in the attempts to represent the Almighty." And even favorable critics felt obliged to apologize for his supposed inability to draw. Not until Roger Fry wrote about him in the *Burlington Magazine* in 1908 was there a critic who understood that his "bad drawing" was actually great design.

In his lifetime he was never to achieve nearly as wide fame as scores of his contemporaries now forgotten. His reputation was confined to a few collectors, critics and fellow artists, who ranked him very high; but to the art world as a whole he remained almost unknown. Indicative of his peculiar position is that in the huge exhibition of American art at the World's Fair in Chicago in 1893, which included fifteen Homers, fifteen Innesses, ten Eakinses, and proportionate numbers of countless minor artists, Ryder was not represented at all.

IV

RYDER WAS completely unworldly. He cared nothing for money, social prestige, or even the ordinary comforts of living. He never married, he lived in disorder, dressed shabbily and ate poorly. He existed only for his art. As he said: "The artist needs but a roof, a crust of bread and his easel, and all the rest God gives him in abundance. He must live to paint and not paint to live. He cannot be a good fellow; he is rarely a wealthy man, and upon the potboiler is inscribed the epitaph of his art." And: "The artist should not sacrifice his ideals to a landlord and a costly studio. A rain-tight roof, frugal living, a box of colors and God's sunlight through clear windows keep the soul attuned and the body vigorous for one's daily work."

Money matters never seemed to worry him. With no responsibilities, not even that of keeping up appearances, he needed little to live on. As usually happens with unworldly people, there was always someone to watch out for him—Cottier, Inglis, Weir, William Macbeth, collector friends like Alexander Morten, Dr. A. T. Sanden or the poet Charles Erskine Scott Wood, or his own brother William, who now ran the Hotel Albert on East Eleventh Street. Weir would sometimes buy his pictures, sell them and give him the profits. Financial affairs were a deep mystery to him. Checks and cash were left lying around his rooms. Once Horatio Walker asked him if he had any money, and Ryder replied that "there was some on a paper in the cupboard." After rummaging around he produced a check in four figures, months old. Walker explained the wisdom of cashing checks and took him to a bank and helped him open an account. Later Ryder told Albert Groll that Walker was not only a fine painter but a great financier.

In the middle 1890's he settled at 308 West Fifteenth Street, which was his home for fifteen years or so. In this drab, crowded neighborhood he had two rooms in an old house, where he lived and worked, without a regular studio—not even a north light. He was utterly unable to cope with housekeeping, and the place soon reached a condition of incredible disorder and dirt. The house agent came once a year to see about repairs and painting, but Ryder would never let him in, so that the rooms were never painted or papered, and rarely cleaned, all the years he was there. Wallpaper hung in long streamers from the ceiling. He never threw anything away, and the rooms were piled waist-high with every conceivable kind of object—furniture, trunks, boxes, old newspapers and magazines, canvases, frames, painting materials, soiled clothes, food, unwashed dishes, milk bottles, ashes. There were paths through this rubbish to the door, to the easel, to the fireplace. Over all lay the dust of years. Ryder did cooking of a kind on an open grate or a small stove, except when he went out for cheap meals in the neighborhood. Being unable to keep his cot clean, he slept on a piece of carpet on the floor.

This was the reality; but he said to Marsden Hartley, "I never see all this unless someone comes to see me." He described how it appeared to him: "I have two windows in my workshop that look out upon an old garden whose great trees thrust their green-laden branches over the casement sills, filtering a network of light and shadow on the bare boards of my floor. Beyond the low roof tops of neighboring houses sweeps the eternal firmament with its ever-changing panorama of mystery and beauty. I would not exchange these two windows for a palace with less a vision than this old garden with its whispering leafage."

In later life Ryder became quite heavy—a big man, with unkempt grizzled hair and full beard, and the face of a seer. In everyday life he wore the clothes of a workman or a tramp—an old sweater, a shabby long overcoat, a fisherman's knitted wool skull-

27

cap. In the evenings he was a familiar figure on Eighth Avenue, walking slowly, his hands behind his back, oblivious of the noise of wagons and streetcars. More than once kindhearted people stopped to give him money. But when he went up to Fifth Avenue "to see the pictures" or when he was invited out to dinner, he wore an old frockcoat or ancient evening clothes and high hat.

He used to walk much around New York, especially at night. On summer evenings when the moon was full he often took the ferry to New Jersey and walked most of the night, returning in the early morning. He told Alexander Shilling that on these walks he "soaked in the moonlight" that reappeared in his pictures. When Captain Robinsin's ship was in port Ryder spent many evenings on board. "On moonlight nights," wrote the Captain, himself an amateur painter, "he would go on to the bridge and watch the numerous craft passing up and down the Hudson. . . . I have known him to walk down to the Battery at midnight, and just sit there studying the effect of clouds passing over the moon, or watching a sailing craft throw the shadow of her sails on the water, or the moonlit ripples where a ferry boat had passed." The Captain cautioned him about walking in the tough waterfront districts, but he said that no one troubled him. "I expect they can see that I have nothing worth stealing about me, and besides, I don't think these people are as bad as they are made out to be."

The New York parks were favorite haunts of his. Olin Warner's daughter Rosalie remembers as a child walking with him in Central Park, and Ryder stopping to look a long time at a vine-covered tree, explaining, "I want to remember it and put it in one of my pictures." He wrote Mrs. Warner in 1897: "I have every faith that my Forest of Arden will be fully as beautiful as any preceding work of mine; Bronx Park has helped me wonderfully, and I would have gone out today for that breezy agitation of nature that is so beautiful, but the rain has spoiled my plans." The critic Sadakichi Hartmann, after trying in vain to see him several times, received a note from Ryder excusing himself for not being in because he had been "absorbing the lovely November skies." It is amusing to con-

28

trast this urban method of gathering landscape data with the average landscape painter's devotion to the country.

Ryder was not only a lover of poetry, he himself composed several poems, which he would often recite to friends or even comparative strangers, and copies of which he used to send as greetings on special occasions such as birthdays or Christmas. They were written with no thought of publication, but a few found their way into print in his lifetime, much to his pleasure. Some were composed to go with particular pictures, and all of them have a fantasy and strangeness that are akin to his painting.

> *The wind, the wind, the wind,*
> *The breath of balmy, balmy evening,*
> *That am I, that am I!*
> *My unseen wanderings*
> *Who can pursue, who comprehend?*

Though marked by the naïveté of the unpractised writer, they often reveal images and phrases that make one feel that if he had devoted his full energy to poetry he might have made a name for himself in that field.

> *Who knows what God knows?*
> *His hand He never shows,*
> *Yet miracles with less are wrought,*
> *Even with a thought.*

Even in old age, when his eccentricities had become extreme, he was not really unsociable. He still saw old friends such as the Weirs, the Warners, the Sanborns, the Lloyd Williams and the Sandens, and his letters to them are full of the warmest affection. He loved children, and those of his friends always received special attention. At Christmas or New Year's he would remember his friends with letters and poems, and for the children he brewed perfume which he put up in little jars. There were also a few new friends among the younger artists, especially Kenneth Hayes Miller and Marsden Hartley, drawn to him by admiration of his art. And even complete strangers could see him in his studio, if they perse-

29

vered. But he was shy of making new friendships. Albert Groll said: "On various occasions I asked him to meet friends of mine, but he always refused. He was courteous about it, but he did not like to meet strangers. He always said, 'Come yourself; you are always welcome, but I don't want to meet any new people.'" This was partly a belief that such contacts detracted from his work; as he put it, "It breaks me up for days when I meet new people."

There was an old-fashioned courtesy about him, not merely formal but based on keen sensibility to others' feelings. If he hated anything it was cruelty in any form. He had an excellent quiet Yankee sense of humor, liked to tell stories, and told them well. On all who knew him, he made an impression of inner harmony and peace.

De Kay wrote that he had "the highest, most chivalrous, but for the most part silent, admiration for women." His poems are full of romantic and often amorous sentiments, but these were probably platonic. There is a story that, hearing a violin being played in his building, he called without introduction on the player, a woman, and asked her to marry him; and his friends, learning of this, packed him off to Europe. If this is true, the cure worked, for Miller said there was no air of being hurt about him. Certainly in any real contest between art and the responsibilities of family life, art would have won.

Among his closest friends in later years were the Fitzpatricks, who lived on the floor below him in the house on West Fifteenth Street. Charles Fitzpatrick was a carpenter, his wife an amateur painter. Ryder and they became fast friends, seeing each other constantly, and he was almost part of their family. Doubtless they supplied some of the domesticity he had lacked for years. Fitzpatrick had been a sailor and had seen much of the world, and the two men would often sing chanties together. When Ryder fell ill the couple took care of him, and while he was helpless Mrs. Fitzpatrick even undertook the heroic job of cleaning out his rooms, much to Ryder's distress.

About 1900, when he was in his early fifties, there came a falling-off in creative ability. After this he originated few if any pictures.

To Miller he said that he could no longer "strike a picture in" as he had when he was younger. This decline, normal in old age, came to Ryder earlier than usual. Perhaps it was due to his mode of life; perhaps it was the penalty of living in a world of fantasy; or perhaps his strange visionary gift, like that of the lyric poet, could not last through mature life. Most of his time was now spent working on paintings already started, in some cases years before. His reluctance to part with his pictures became intensified almost to the point of mania. *Macbeth and the Witches* (plate 73), *The Race Track* (plate 69), *Desdemona* (plate 60) and *The Lorelei* (plate 76) remained for years in his studio. *The Tempest* (plate 68), exhibited as early as 1891, was still being painted on almost up to his death. Sometimes he even borrowed pictures back from the owners, and worked more on them. Because of his failing powers they were seldom improved in the process.

By this time there was a demand for his work, though still from a limited number of collectors. At the Clarke sale in 1899 *The Temple of the Mind* had sold for $2,250 and *Christ Appearing to Mary* for $1,000—prices that established the financial soundness of his work. There was now a waiting list for his paintings, and several had been paid for in advance. In most cases the buyers had to wait years to get them. Of one such purchaser he said to Walter Pach, "I was worried somewhat at first by his wanting to take his picture away before I had finished, but lately he has been very nice about it—only comes around once a year or so." His letters of the time show much anxiety over his difficulty in finishing. "I sometimes think," he wrote in 1903, "the smallest thing I do, it is as if my life depended on it; and then the great shadow, always, of the impossible and the unattainable."

The growing esteem of the younger generation was shown by the inclusion of six paintings by him in the Armory Show of 1913. On the other hand, an unpleasant by-product of the demand for his work and the limited supply, was the number of forgeries that were already appearing in his last years. In 1915 he wrote Alexander Morten, who owned fourteen of his pictures: "I rarely sign my paintings, having always felt that they spoke for themselves; but

31

. . . I am sorry to say, a great many spurious Ryders have lately come into the market," and then went on to authenticate Morten's pictures. After his death the production of "Ryders" became a steady industry, until today there are about five times as many forgeries as genuine works.

In 1915 Ryder had a serious illness and spent four months in a hospital. When he came out the Fitzpatricks took him to live with them, and it was in their house in Elmhurst, Long Island, that he died, March 28, 1917, nine days after his seventieth birthday.

Ryder's art was remote from the prevailing spirit of his time, with its naturalism, preoccupation with outdoor color and sunlight, and shunning of "literary" subject-matter. Though he had always had a small circle of appreciators, wider recognition came only after his death, and was linked to the rise of the modern movement. It then became apparent how prophetic he was of certain tendencies of modern art—in his freedom from bondage to literal naturalism, his relation to the unconscious mind, and his expression of ideas and emotions in purely plastic language. Today his art seems more contemporary to us than it did to his own generation.

1. *Self-portrait*. Canvas mounted on wood, 6½ x 5″. Collection Mr. and Mrs. Lawrence A. Fleischman

2. *The Curfew Hour.* Wood, 7½ x 10¾". The Metropolitan Museum of Art, Rogers Fund, 1909

3. *The Sheepfold.* Canvas 8½ x 10½". In the Brooklyn Museum Collection, Gift of A. A. Healy

4. *Mending the Harness*. Canvas, 19 x 22⅝″. National Gallery of Art, Gift of Sam A. Lewisohn

5. *Spring*. Canvas, 14¼ x 18¾". The Toledo Museum of Art, Gift of Florence Scott Libbey, 1923

6. *Evening Glow—The Old Red Cow*. Canvas, 7¾ x 9″. In the Brooklyn Museum Collection, Loeser Art Fund

7. *The Barnyard*. Wood, 11½ x 12″. Munson-Williams-Proctor Institute

8. *Grazing Horse.* Canvas, 10¼ x 14³⁄₁₆″. In the Brooklyn Museum Collection

9. *Summer's Fruitful Pasture*. Wood, 7¾ x 9⅞". In the Brooklyn Museum Collection

10. *Dancing Dryads*. Canvas, 9 x 7". National Collection of Fine Arts

11. *Pegasus, or The Poet on Pegasus Entering the Realm of the Muses.* Wood, 12 x 11⅜".
Worcester Art Museum

12. *The Lovers' Boat, or Moonlight on the Waters.* Wood, 11⅜ x 12″. Guennol Collection

13. *The Wood Road.* Canvas, 6¼ x 6⅞″. Collection Dr. Loring H. Dodd

14. *Gay Head*. Canvas, 7½ x 12¾". The Phillips Collection, Washington

15. *The Pasture*, Canvas, 12⅞ x 15¼″. Collection Dr. C. J. Robertson

16. *The Windmill*. Canvas, 16 x 14". Guennol Collection

17. *Toilers of the Sea.* Wood, 11⅜ x 12″. The Metropolitan Museum of Art, George A. Hearn Fund, 1915

18. *Sunset Hour.* Canvas, 10 x 13". Collection Mr. Stephen C. Clark

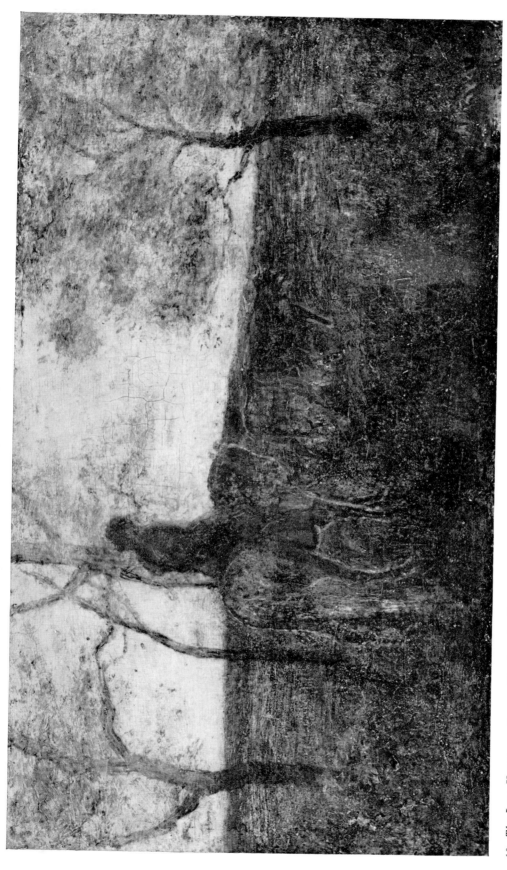

19. *The Lone Horseman.* Composition board, 7¹⁵⁄₁₆ x 14½". Guennol Collection

20. *The Lovers*. Wood, 11⁷⁄₁₆ x 7¾″. Vassar College Art Gallery

21. *Roadside Meeting*. Canvas, 15¾₁₆ x 12⁷₁₆″. The Butler Institute of American Art

22. *The Pond*. Canvas. 12¼ x 16½″. Walker Art Center

23. *The White Horse.* Canvas, 8⅛ x 10″. The Art Museum, Princeton University

24. *A Country Girl*. Canvas, 9½ x 5¾″. Randolph-Macon Woman's College

25. *Moonlight Marine*. Wood, 11⅜ x 12″. The Metropolitan Museum of Art, Samuel D. Lee Fund, 1934

26. *Pastoral Study*. Canvas, 24¼ x 29½". National Collection of Fine Arts

27. *In the Stable.* Canvas, 21 x 32″. National Collection of Fine Arts

28. *Homeward Bound.* Canvas mounted on wood, 8⅞ x 18". The Phillips Collection, Washington

29. *The Dead Bird.* Wood, 4¼ x 9⅞". The Phillips Collection, Washington

30. *Resurrection*. Canvas, 17⅛ x 14⅛″. The Phillips Collection, Washington

31. *With Sloping Mast and Dipping Prow.* Canvas, 12 x 11¼″. National Collection of Fine Arts

32. *Moonlight on the Sea.* Wood, 11½ x 15⅞". Roland P. Murdock Collection, Wichita Art Museum

33. *Christ Appearing to Mary*. Canvas, 14¼ x 17½". National Collection of Fine Arts

34. *Moonrise, Marine.* Canvas, 9¼ x 11⅛". Guennol Collection

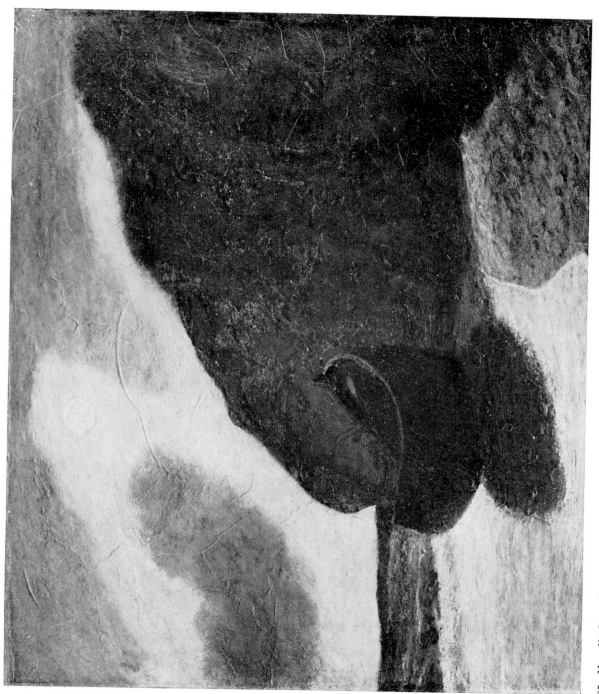

35. *Moonlit Cove*. Canvas, 14⅛ x 17⅛". The Phillips Collection, Washington

36. *The Temple of the Mind.* From an early photograph

37. *The Temple of the Mind*. Wood, 17¹³⁄₁₆ x 15¹⁵⁄₁₆". Albright Art Gallery

38. Detail from *The Temple of the Mind*

39. *Hunter's Rest*. Canvas, 14½ x 24¼″. Collection Mr. and Mrs. Lawrence A. Fleischman

41. *The Sea, or Lord Ullin's Daughter*. Canvas, 20⅜ x 18½". National Collection of Fine Arts

42. *By the Tomb of the Prophet*. Wood, 5 13/16 x 11 7/16″. Collection Mr. and Mrs. Lawrence A. Fleischman

43. *Oriental Camp*. Canvas, 7¼ x 12″. Amherst College

44. *Moonlight*. Wood, 11⁷⁄₁₆ x 12¹⁄₁₆″. In the Brooklyn Museum Collection, Gift of Mr. and Mrs. Solton Engel

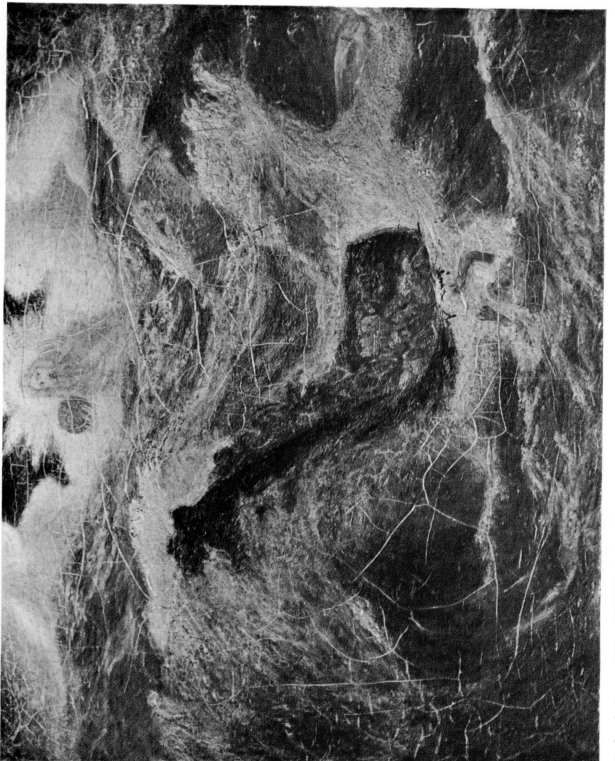

45. *Jonah*. Canvas, 27⅛ x 34⅜". National Collection of Fine Arts

46. *The Lone Scout*. Canvas, 13¼ x 10⅛″. Collection Mr. T. E. Hanley

47. *The Sentimental Journey.* Canvas, 12 x 10″. Canajoharie Library and Art Gallery

48. *Under a Cloud.* Canvas, 20 x 24″. Collection Mrs. T. Durland Van Orden

49. TOP: *Shore Scene*. Canvas, 9½ x 27¼″. Georgia Museum of Art
50. BOTTOM: *The Smugglers' Cove*. Gilded leather, 10 x 28″. The Metropolitan Museum of Art, Rogers Fund, 1909

51. *A Stag Drinking*. Gilded leather. 27 x 19⅛″. Collection Mr. George B. Berger, Jr.

52. *A Stag and Two Does.* Gilded leather, 27 x 19″. Collection Mr. George B. Berger, Jr.

53. *Diana*. Gilded leather, 28¾ x 19⅞". Collection Dr. John Mayers

54. *The Flying Dutchman*. Canvas, 14¼ x 17¼". National Collection of Fine Arts

55. *Perrette.* Canvas mounted on wood, 12⅞ x 7¾″. Smith College Museum of Art

56. *Marine*. Canvas, 12⅝ x 9¹³⁄₁₆″. Collection Mr. Leo M. Rogers

57. *Joan of Arc.* Canvas, 10⅛ x 7⅛″. Worcester Art Museum

58. *The Story of the Cross*. Canvas, 14 x 11⅜". Guennol Collection

59. *The Shepherdess*. Wood, 10⅛ x 6⅞". In the Brooklyn Museum Collection, Loeser Art Fund

60. *Desdemona*. Canvas, 14⅛ x 10⅛". The Phillips Collection, Washington

61. Detail from *Siegfried and the Rhine Maidens*

62. *Siegfried and the Rhine Maidens*. Canvas, 19¾ x 20½". National Gallery of Art

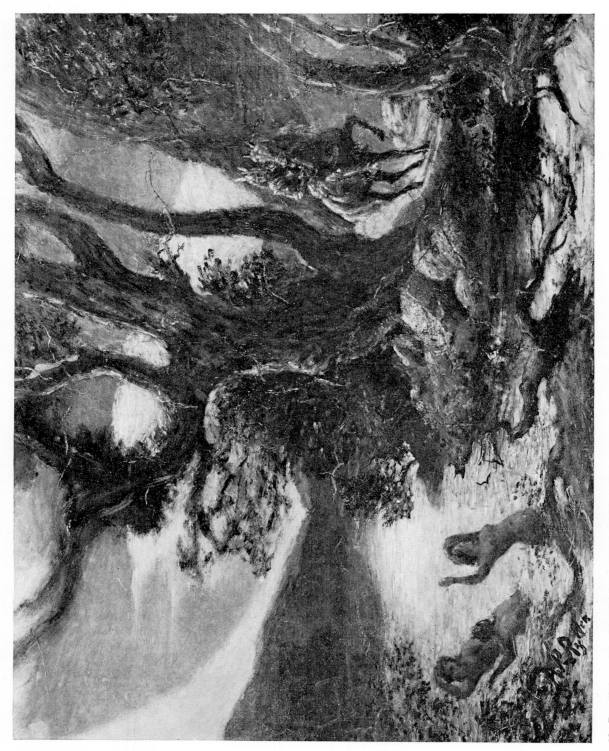

63. Detail from *Siegfried and the Rhine Maidens*

64. Detail from *Siegfried and the Rhine Maidens*

65. *Constance*. Canvas, 28¼ x 35¾". Museum of Fine Arts, Boston

66. *Constance*. From an early photograph

67. Detail from *Constance*

68. *The Tempest*. Canvas, 27½ x 35″. Detroit Institute of Arts

69. *The Race Track.* Canvas, 27¾" x 35⅝". Cleveland Museum of Art, J. H. Wade Collection

70. *The Race Track*. From an early photograph

71. Detail from *The Race Track*

72. *The Canal.* Canvas, 18 x 24″. Arizona State College

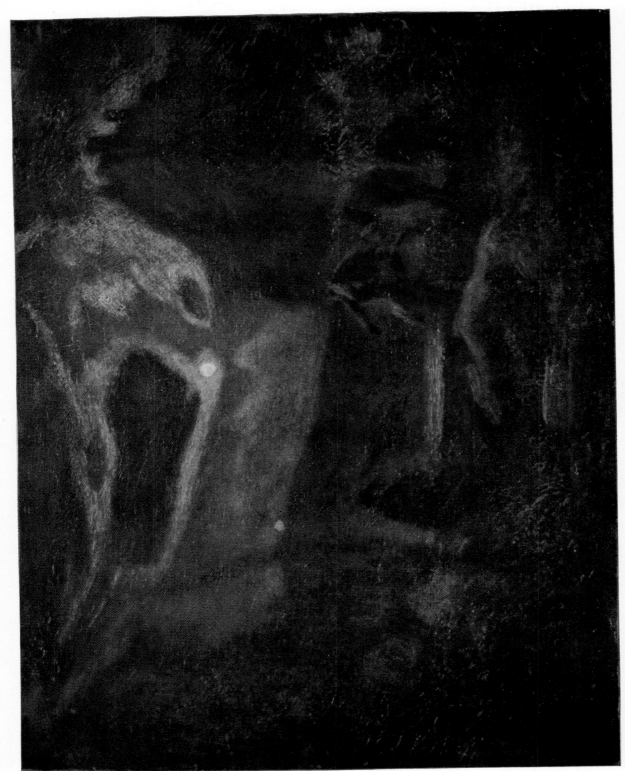

72. *Macbeth and the Witches*. Canvas, 28⅛ x 35¾". The Phillips Collection, Washington

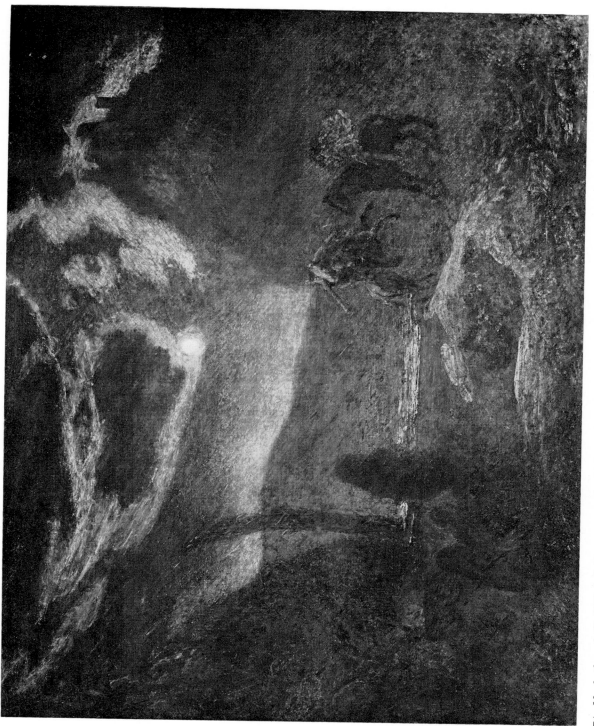

74. *Macbeth and the Witches.* From an early photograph

75. Detail from *Macbeth and the Witches*

76. *The Lorelei*. Canvas, 22½ x 19¼". Guennol Collection

77. Detail from *The Forest of Arden*

78. *The Forest of Arden.* Canvas, 19 x 15″. Collection Mr. Stephen C. Clark

79. *Passing Song*. Wood, 8½ x 4⅝″. National Collection of Fine Arts

80. *King Cophetua and the Beggar Maid.* Canvas, 24½ x 18″. National Collection of Fine Arts

81. *Weir's Orchard.* Canvas, 17⅞″ x 21″. Collection Mr. T. E. Hanley

NOTES ON THE ILLUSTRATIONS

THE ORDER of the illustrations is generally chronological. Ryder never dated his paintings, and he often worked on them for years, even after they were exhibited or sold. His pictures were relatively little shown, reproduced or referred to in his lifetime. Hence the exact chronology of his works cannot be determined. However, certain pictures—about a third of those illustrated here—can be at least approximately dated by contemporary records of exhibition, sale or published reference. The balance have been arranged by their relation to the foregoing. The dating is by the time of conception, not of completion.

In most cases, the earliest clear photograph available has been used, to show the picture in as good condition as possible. A number of the photographs are from negatives made by the Metropolitan Museum of Art in 1918.

1. *Self-portrait.* Probably early 1880's.
2. *The Curfew Hour.* Exhibited 1882.
3. *The Sheepfold.* Probably late 1870's.
5. *Spring.* Illustrated in 1880.
10. *Dancing Dryads.* Exhibited in 1881. Ryder wrote this poem for it:

    In the morning; ashen-hued,
    Came nymphs dancing through the wood.

11. *Pegasus.* Ryder was working on this in 1883. Inscribed on back: "Painted by Albert P. Ryder for Charles de Kay 1887." De Kay in his article on Ryder in 1890 gave the title as "The Poet on Pegasus Entering the Realm of the Muses."

113

12. *The Lovers' Boat.* Exhibited in 1881, with this poem:

> *In splendor rare, the moon,*
> *In full-orbed splendor,*
> *On sea and darkness making light,*
> *While windy spaces and night,*
> *In all vastness, did make,*
> *With cattled hill and lake,*
> *A scene grand and lovely.*
> *Then, gliding above the*
> *Dark water, a lover's boat,*
> *In quiet beauty, did float*
> *Upon the scene, mingling shadows*
> *Into the deeper shadows*
> *Of sky and land reflected.*

17. *Toilers of the Sea.* Exhibited in 1884, with this poem:

> *'Neath the shifting skies,*
> *O'er the billowy foam,*
> *The hardy fisher flies*
> *To his island home.*

21. *Roadside Meeting.* Given by Ryder to his mother.

28. *Homeward Bound.* Painted by Ryder for his friend Captain John Robinson about 1893–94.

30. *Resurrection.* Finished in 1885, sold that year, illustrated in 1886.

33. *Christ Appearing to Mary.* Bought by Thomas B. Clarke in April 1885.

37. *The Temple of the Mind.* Bought by Thomas B. Clarke in April 1885. Ryder wrote Prof. John Pickard in 1907: "The theme is Poe's Haunted Palace. . . . The finer attributes of the mind are pictured by three graces who stand in the centre of the picture: where their shadows from the moonlight fall toward the spectator. They are waiting for a weeping love to join them. On the left is a Temple where a cloven footed faun dances up the steps snapping his fingers in fiendish glee at having dethroned the erstwhile ruling graces." Comparison with Poe's poem *The Haunted Palace,* which appears in *The Fall of the House of Usher,* shows how freely Ryder interpreted the theme.

40. *Moonlight.* Painted on the back of the same panel as *The Temple of the Mind,* and later sawed apart.

41. *The Sea, or Lord Ullin's Daughter.* Based on Thomas Campbell's poem, *Lord Ullin's Daughter.*

42. *By the Tomb of the Prophet.* This, *Oriental Camp, The Lone Scout* and a few others were probably inspired by Ryder's visit to Tangier in 1882.

45. *Jonah*. Ryder's letter of April 1885 to Thomas B. Clarke: "I am in ecstasys over my Jonah: such a lovely turmoil of boiling water and everything. . . . If I get the scheme of color that haunts me: I think you will be delighted with it." First exhibited in 1890. Illustrated in 1890, showing major differences from the present picture.

47. *The Sentimental Journey*. Sold in April 1889.

51 and 52. *A Stag Drinking* and *A Stag and Two Does*. Two panels of a three-panel screen: the center panel, *Beech Trees Near a Pool*, was by Homer D. Martin (1836–1897). Ryder painted a number of such decorated screens, probably for Cottier & Co.

54. *The Flying Dutchman*. Based on Wagner's opera. Exhibited in 1887.

55. *Perrette*. Based on Fables of La Fontaine, Book 7, Fable 10. The milkmaid Perrette, walking with a pail of milk on her head, dreamed of how she would use the money the milk would bring, and in the joy of anticipation spilt the milk. Painted by 1890; exhibited in 1891.

57. *Joan of Arc*. Sold in 1889. Ryder wrote a poem for it; the first stanza reads:

> *On a rude mossy throne*
> *Made by Nature in the stone*
> *Joan sits; and her eyes far away*
> *Rest upon the mountains gray.*
> *And far beyond the moving clouds*
> *That wrap the sky in vap'rous shrouds,*
> *Visions, she sees—*
> *And voices come to her on the breeze.*

58. *The Story of the Cross*. This or another version of the same subject were begun several years before 1890.

60. *Desdemona*. Based on Shakespeare's *Othello*. Ryder wrote J. Alden Weir in 1896: "I have finished Desdemona."

62. *Siegfried and the Rhine Maidens*. Based on Wagner's *Götterdämmerung*. Elliott Daingerfield wrote in 1918 that Ryder told him: "I had been to hear the opera and went home about twelve o'clock and began this picture. I worked for forty-eight hours without sleep or food, and the picture was the result." The depth of pigment, however, indicates that he worked further on it. Exhibited in 1891.

65. *Constance*. Based on Chaucer's *Canterbury Tales, The Man of Law's Tale*. Constance, daughter of the emperor of Rome and wife of the king of Northumberland, was treacherously cast adrift with her infant son in a ship without sail or rudder, but was miraculously safeguarded and after five years on the sea reached Rome. Ryder wrote Weir in 1896: "I have finished . . . Constance." Plates 66 and 67 are from a photograph taken about 1905.

115

68. *The Tempest.* Based on Shakespeare's *The Tempest,* Act I, Scene II; Prospero, Miranda and Caliban. Exhibited in 1891, but worked on further. Ryder wrote Weir in 1896: "I have a good grip on Tempest," but he labored over it for years, and it remained in his possession until his death.

69. *The Race Track.* Of its genesis Ryder wrote that a waiter whom he knew in his brother's hotel, The Albert, lost his life's savings on a horse race, and committed suicide. "This fact formed a cloud over my mind that I could not throw off, and 'The Race Track' is the result." The race was probably in 1888; the first known record of the painting was about 1895; Ryder continued to work on it until about 1910. Plates 70 and 71 are from a photograph taken in 1918, before the picture was restored in the 1920's.

73. *Macbeth and the Witches.* Based on Shakespeare's *Macbeth,* Act I, Scene III. Begun probably before 1895; worked on for fifteen to twenty years. Plates 74 and 75 are from a photograph taken about 1913, before the painting was restored in the 1920's.

76. *The Lorelei.* Ryder wrote Weir in 1896: "I have finished ... Lorelei." But he continued to work on it for years and it remained in his possession until his death.

78. *The Forest of Arden.* Based on Shakespeare's *As You Like It.* Finished in 1897.

79. *Passing Song.* Being worked on in the late 1890's and early 1900's. Ryder wrote a poem for it, beginning: "By a deep, flowing river, / There is a maiden pale, / And her ruby lips quiver / A song on the gale." The poem tells of a youth floating past, down the river, echoing her song, but: "Alas there's no rudder / To the ship that he sails;" he drifts out to sea, and she will die of grief.

80. *King Cophetua and the Beggar Maid.* Based on *Percy's Reliques of Ancient English Poetry,* Series I, Book II. Cophetua, king of Africa, "disdained all womankind," but one day saw a beggar-girl, fell in love with her, and made her his queen. Ryder was working on this in 1900.

81. *Weir's Orchard.* J. Alden Weir's farm at Branchville, Conn., which Ryder often visited.

116

A NOTE ON FORGERIES

RYDER HAS BEEN more widely forged than any American artist except Blakelock. His small production, the fact that he originated few pictures in his last fifteen or twenty years, his growing reputation among collectors, and the fairly high prices his works brought in his old age, attracted forgers even during his lifetime; and the production of fakes grew steadily after his death. Although he painted only about a hundred and sixty pictures, there are probably five times as many falsely ascribed to him. The fakers specialized in moonlit marines, based on the two most accessible paintings of this type, *Toilers of the Sea* (plate 17) and *Moonlight Marine* (plate 25) in the Metropolitan Museum. But in the end they so confused things that they no longer knew Ryder's style, and imitated each other. Many "Ryders" in the market today, as well as some in museums and private collections, have only a remote relation to his work.

In order to clarify this situation, I started over twenty years ago to gather all available information on Ryder's life and works, to be published in a catalogue raisonné. The first step was to establish which works could be proved genuine by objective evidence, such as an unbroken history of ownership going back to the artist, or records of the picture during his lifetime (exhibitions, reproductions, descriptions or other published references). A thorough examination was made of published material since 1865—books, magazines, newspaper reviews, exhibition and auction catalogues. Records of dealers who had handled his work during his lifetime were consulted. Every such bit of information was entered under each picture. This established that over a hundred works were recorded during Ryder's life in such ways as to prove their authenticity.

These works were subjected to thorough study, using x-ray, microscopic examination and examination under ultra-violet light. This study was carried on chiefly in the laboratory of the Brooklyn Museum, with

117

Toilers of the Sea. The Metropolitan Museum of Art.

Radiograph of *Toilers of the Sea.*

A typical forged Ryder marine.

Radiograph of the forged marine.

the invaluable help of Sheldon Keck, the Museum's technical expert. It resulted in a more complete knowledge of Ryder's style and technique than had been possible before.

On the basis of this knowledge, the same intensive study was made of several hundred pictures which did not have objective evidence of authenticity. A certain proportion of these were found to have stylistic and technical qualities characteristic of Ryder, so that they could be accepted as his work. A very much larger proportion were found to have characteristics completely different from Ryder's. The difference between the two classes was clear and definite.

X-ray was particularly useful in this study. A radiograph (x-ray photograph) makes it possible to see beneath the surface of a painting into its inner structure. The x-rays penetrate most substances to varying degrees, but are stopped by certain substances. White lead is a good deal more resistant than most other pigments, so what the radiograph shows is chiefly the white lead content. The whites in the radiograph are areas of thick white lead, the darks are areas of less resistant pigments—not necessarily where the paint is thinner but where it contains less lead. Since a painter usually creates lights with white lead or zinc white, the radiograph corresponds in a general way with the lights and darks in the painting.

Ryder worked long over his pictures, building them up in layer upon layer of pigments and glazes, often modifying the forms. Hence in his radiographs the forms do not visualize sharply, the edges are often blurred, and few details are clear. The effect is rather like a composite photograph. But the radiographs almost always show the main areas of white lead and of translucent pigments, the former relatively dense and visualizing as almost pure white, the latter dark. Thus they usually reveal the general structure of Ryder's compositions and the way they were built up.

The forgers, on the other hand, paint simply and directly, trying to simulate Ryder's long laborious processes by short-cut methods which are clearly revealed by the x-ray. Radiographs of forgeries generally show little more than a heavy blank undersurface, thinly painted over. Even when some of the composition visualizes, the thin direct technique can be distinguished from Ryder's rich and complicated processes.

Scientific examination, of course, has not been the only factor taken into account. The determination of authenticity or falsity depends on balancing many different kinds of evidence—old records, history, style, technique. By assembling and studying all these different forms of evidence, I have endeavored to clarify the confusion caused by forgers, and to restore the life work of a great artist.

120

CHRONOLOGICAL NOTE

ALBERT PINKHAM RYDER was born in New Bedford, Massachusetts, March 19, 1847. He began painting landscapes, without regular instruction. About 1870 he moved to New York, his home for the rest of his life. He studied for a time at the National Academy of Design, but more important was the informal teaching of William E. Marshall, portraitist and engraver. Ryder's early works were landscapes, often with figures or with horses, cows and sheep, small in scale and more naturalistic in style than his later works. His first recorded exhibition was at the National Academy in 1873, but he was shown there only once in the next seven years. About 1875 he and four other painters held an exhibition at Cottier & Co., which aroused interest and led to the founding in 1877 of the Society of American Artists, of which Ryder was one of twenty-two founders, and in which he exhibited from 1878 to 1887.

His first trip abroad was in 1877, for a month in London. In the summer of 1882 he and Daniel Cottier toured England; then, joined by the sculptor Olin Warner, they visited France, Holland, Italy, Spain and Tangier, not remaining long in any country. In 1887 and 1896 Ryder crossed and re-crossed the Atlantic on his friend Captain Robinson's ships, spending a short time in London.

After about 1880 Ryder embarked on more imaginative themes. From the early and middle 1880's date some of his most important works, such as *Pegasus, The Temple of the Mind, Christ Appearing to Mary, Resurrection, Jonah, The Flying Dutchman* and *The Story of the Cross.* The later 1880's and the 1890's saw the beginnings of *Siegfried, The Tempest, Constance, The Race Track, Macbeth and the Witches* and *The Forest of Arden.* Most of these pictures were worked on for years, and some remained in his possession until his death. After

121

1887 he exhibited seldom except when works were lent by collectors to shows in the New York clubs. The first important article on him appeared in 1890 in *The Century,* written by Charles de Kay. About 1900 there came a falling-off in creative ability, and after this he originated few pictures.

In the mid-1890's he settled at 308 West Fifteenth Street, and that remained his home for fifteen or more years. In 1915 he had a serious illness, spending four months in a hospital; and then went to live with his friends Mr. and Mrs. Charles Fitzpatrick in Elmhurst, Long Island, where he died on March 28, 1917.

SELECTED BIBLIOGRAPHY

The place of publication is New York unless otherwise noted.

Monographs

Price, Frederic Newlin: *Ryder,* 1932. 71 il.
Sherman, Frederic Fairchild: *Albert Pinkham Ryder,* 1920. 33 il.

Books and Exhibition Catalogues

Barker, Virgil: *American Painting,* 1950. 4 il.
Baur, John I. H.: *American Painting in the Nineteenth Century,* 1953. 1 il.
————— *Revolution and Tradition in Modern American Art,* Cambridge, Mass., 1951. 2 il.
Burroughs, Alan: *Limners and Likenesses,* Cambridge, Mass., 1936. 2 il.
Caffin, Charles H.: *The Story of American Painting,* 1907. 2 il.
Cahill, Holger; and Barr, Alfred H., Jr.: *Art in America in Modern Times,* 1934. 4 il.
Cook, Clarence: *Art and Artists of Our Time,* v. 3, 1888. 1 il.
Cortissoz, Royal: *American Artists,* 1923. 1 il.
Craven, Thomas: *Men of Art,* 1931. 1 il.
Eliot, Alexander: *Three Hundred Years of American Painting,* 1957. 5 il.
Flexner, James Thomas: *The Pocket History of American Painting,* 1950. 1 il.
Hartley, Marsden: *Adventures in the Arts,* 1921.
Hartmann, Sadakichi: *A History of American Art,* Boston, Mass., 1902, v. 1. 1 il.
Isham, Samuel: *The History of American Painting,* 1936. 1 il.
LaFollette, Suzanne: *Art in America,* 1929. 2 il.
Larkin, Oliver W.: *Art and Life in America,* 1949. 1 il.
Mather, Frank Jewett, Jr.: *Estimates in Art,* 1931.
Mather, Frank Jewett, Jr.; Morey, Charles Rufus; Henderson, William James: *The Pageant of America.* "The American Spirit in Art," New Haven, Conn., 1927. 5 il.

The Metropolitan Museum of Art: *Loan Exhibition of the Works of Albert P. Ryder*, introduction by Bryson Burroughs, 1918. 48 il.

Morris, Harrison S.: *Confessions in Art*, 1930.

Mumford, Lewis: *The Brown Decades*, 1931. 1 il.

The Museum of Modern Art, N. Y.: *Romantic Painting in America*, by James Thrall Soby and Dorothy C. Miller, 1943. 3 il.

———— *Homer, Ryder, Eakins*, 1930, "Albert Pinkham Ryder" by Bryson Burroughs. 9 il.

National Cyclopaedia of American Biography, v. 10, 1900. 2 il.

Phillips, Duncan: *The Artist Sees Differently*, 1931. 7 il.

———— *A Collection in the Making*, 1926. 4 il.

Richardson, E. P.: *Painting in America*, 1956. 2 il.

Robb, David M.: *The Harper History of Painting*, 1951. 1 il.

Rosenfeld, Paul: *Port of New York*, 1924. 1 il.

Sherman, Frederick Fairchild: *Landscape and Figure Painters of America*, 1917. 4 il.

Julian Alden Weir, ed. by J. B. Millet, 1921, p. 71, 104–106, 119–120.

Whitney Museum of American Art: *Albert P. Ryder Centenary Exhibition*, by Lloyd Goodrich, 1947. 16 il.

Periodicals

Baldinger, W. S.: "Art of Eakins, Homer and Ryder: A Social Revaluation," *Art Quarterly*, v. 9, Summer 1946, p. 213–233.

Barker, Virgil: "Albert Pinkham Ryder," *Creative Art*, v. 5, Dec. 1929, p. 838–842. 5 il.

Beck, Walter de S.: "Albert Pinkham Ryder: An Appreciation," *International Studio*, v. 70, Apr. 1920, p. xxxvii–xlvi. 6 il.

Braddock, Richard: "The Literary World of Albert Pinkham Ryder," *Gazette des Beaux-Arts*, v. 33, Jan. 1948, p. 47–54. 8 il.

Coates, Robert M.: "The Art Galleries," *New Yorker*, Nov. 1, 1947, p. 80, 82–83.

Daingerfield, Elliott: "Albert Pinkham Ryder, Artist and Dreamer," *Scribner's Magazine*, v. 63, Mar. 1918, p. 380–384. 2 il.

Eckford, Henry [Charles de Kay]: "A Modern Colorist, Albert Pinkham Ryder," *Century Magazine*, v. 40, June 1890. 4 il.

French, Joseph Lewis: "A Painter of Dreams," *Broadway Magazine*, v. 14, Sept. 1905, p. 3–9. 7 il.

Fry, Roger E.: "The Art of Albert P. Ryder," *Burlington Magazine*, v. 13, Apr. 1908, p. 63–64. 5 il.

Goodrich, Lloyd: "Realism and Romanticism in Homer, Eakins and Ryder," *Art Quarterly*, v. 12, Winter 1949, p. 26–28. 2 il.

———— "What Is American in American Art?" *Art in America*, v. 46, Fall 1958, p. 24–25. 1 il.

Hartley, Marsden: "Albert P. Ryder," *The Seven Arts*, v. 2, May 1917, p. 93–96.

Hartmann, Sadakichi: "Albert Pinkham Ryder," *Magazine of Art*, v. 31, Sept. 1938, p. 500–503, 550. 4 il.

—— "A Visit to A. P. Ryder!" *Art News*, v. 1, Mar. 1897, p. 1–3.

Hyde, William H.: "Albert Ryder as I Knew Him," *The Arts*, v. 16, May 1930, p. 596–599. 2 il.

Lane, James W.: "A View of Two Native Romantics," *Art News*, v. 38, Nov. 11, 1939, p. 9, 16. 1 il.

Louchheim, Aline B.: "Ryder Seen by Marsden Hartley, Walt Kuhn, Yasuo Kuniyoshi, Reginald Marsh, Kenneth Hayes Miller," *Art News*, v. 46, Nov. 1947, p. 28–31. 6 il.

W. M. M. [William M. Milliken]: "*The Race Track*, or *Death on a Pale Horse* by Albert Pinkham Ryder," *Cleveland Museum of Art Bulletin*, v. 15, Mar. 1928, p. 65–71. 1 il.

"The Marines of Albert P. Ryder," *Art in America*, v. 8, Dec. 1919, p. 28–32. 1 il.

Mather, Frank Jewett, Jr.: "The Romantic Spirit in American Art," *Nation*, v. 104, Apr. 12, 1917, p. 427.

—— "Albert Pinkham Ryder's Beginnings," *Art in America*, v. 9, Apr. 1921, p. 119–127. 4 il.

Pach, Walter: "On Albert P. Ryder," *Scribner's Magazine*, v. 49, Jan. 1911, p. 125–128. 3 il.

Phillips, Duncan: "Albert Ryder," *American Magazine of Art*, v. 7, Aug. 1916, p. 387–391. 4 il.

Price, F. Newlin: "Albert Pinkham Ryder," *International Studio*, v. 81, July 1925, p. 282–288. 10 il.

Robinson, John: "Personal Reminiscences of Albert Pinkham Ryder," *Art in America*, v. 13, June 1925, p. 176, 179–187. 3 il.

Rosenfeld, Paul: "American Painting," *Dial*, v. 71, Dec. 1921, p. 649–655. 1 il.

Ryder, Albert P.: "Paragraphs from the Studio of a Recluse," *Broadway Magazine*, v. 14, Sept. 1905, p. 10–11. 1 il.

"Albert Pinkham Ryder—Painter," *The Index of Twentieth Century Artists*, v. 1, no. 5, Feb. 1934, p. 65–72, sup. i, iii, v.

"Albert P. Ryder's *Jonah*," *Art in America*, v. 8, Feb. 1920, p. 81–82. 1 il.

Sargeant, Winthrop: "Nocturnal Genius," *Life*, v. 30, Feb. 26, 1951, p. 87–96, 101–102. 14 il.

Schnakenberg, H. E.,: "Albert P. Ryder," *The Arts*, v. 6, Nov. 1924, p. 271–275. 2 il.

Sherman, Frederic Fairchild: "Notes on the Art of Albert P. Ryder," *Art in America*, v. 25, Oct. 1937, p. 167–173. 5 il.

—— "Paintings Erroneously Attributed to Albert Pinkham Ryder," *Art in America*, v. 25, Apr. 1937, p. 87–89.

—— "Some Likenesses of Albert Pinkham Ryder," *Art in America*, v. 26, Jan. 1938, p. 32–33, 35. 7 il.

—— "Some Paintings by Albert Pinkham Ryder," *Art in America*, v. 5, Apr. 1917, p. 155–162. 4 il.

—— "Some Paintings Erroneously Attributed to Albert Pinkham Ryder," *Art in America*, v. 24, Oct. 1936, p. 160–161.

—— "Two Marines by Albert P. Ryder," *Art in America*, v. 12, Oct. 1924, p. 296–300. 2 il.

——— "Two Unpublished Paintings by Albert Pinkham Ryder," *Art in America,* v. 14, Dec. 1925, p. 23–25. 1 il.

——— "Unpublished Paintings by Albert Pinkham Ryder," *Art in America,* v. 8, Apr. 1920, p. 129–137. 4 il.

Stein, Leo: "Albert Ryder," *New Republic,* v. 14, Apr. 27, 1918, p. 385–386.

Weller, Allen: "An Unpublished Letter by Albert P. Ryder," *Art in America,* v. 27, Apr. 1939, p. 101–102. 1 il.

PHOTOGRAPHIC CREDITS

The photographs in this book are reproduced through the courtesy of those listed below:

Albright Art Gallery   37
Babcock Galleries   22, 46, 56
Ferdinand Boesch   58
Brenwasser Photographer   24, 32
Brooklyn Museum   3, 6, 8, 9, 59
Butler Institute of American Art   21
Cleveland Museum   69, 71
Detroit Institute of Arts   68
Lawrence A. Fleischman   7
Peter A. Juley & Son   15, 48, 74, 75
Sheldon Keck   87
M. Knoedler & Co.   7, 10, 15, 18
Life Magazine   33, 48
Guennol Collection   19, 23, 76
Dr. John Mayers   53
Metropolitan Museum of Art   2, 4, 11, 14, 20, 25, 26, 27, 34, 35, 41, 44, 50, 70, 79, 80
Milch Art Gallery   12, 39, 49, 72
National Collection of Fine Arts   31, 40
National Gallery of Art   61, 62, 63, 64
Philadelphia Museum of Art   16
Phillips Collection, Washington   28, 29, 30, 60, 73
Sandak, Inc.   45, 54, 65, 78
Time, Inc.   17
Toledo Museum of Art   5
Whitney Museum of American Art   1, 13, 36, 38, 43, 55, 66, 81
Worcester Museum   57

INDEX

The roman numerals refer to text references, the *italic* numerals to the black and white plates, and the **bold face** numerals to the color plates. The titles of the reproductions are listed in *italics*.

127

128